the still point
Katherine Moss

Dedicated to Eileen and Tony Moss.

For Isabelle.

VERVE
POETRY PRESS
BIRMINGHAM

PUBLISHED BY VERVE POETRY PRESS
https://vervepoetrypress.com
mail@vervepoetrypress.com

FIRST PUBLISHED NOV 2023

Printed and bound in the UK
by Imprint Digital, Exeter

ISBN: 978-1-913917-41-8

CONTENTS

Acknowledgements

Katherine Moss is a poet and SEN teaching assistant based in Manchester. Their writing explores the intersection of truth and familial lore, particularly within the Irish Diaspora. Katherine's work examines contemporary and historical lived experience of the Working Class. Their monologue, 'Linda's Shield' was produced by The Garrick Theatre online in 2020. The story reflected the impact of high COVID-19 mortality rates on disabled people in the UK. 'The Stonemason's List', a short story, was published in the Comma Press Anthology, 'Mounds of Millet' in 2023. *The Still Point* is Katherine's debut pamphlet.

St Francis' satyr

Place it on the scales
a dial quivers, rests at nought
it weighs nothing
makes you look foolish.

Place it in your palm
this puzzling insubstantial mass.
Pass it from hand to hand
like a burning morsel.

Place it on the ground
it is destined to defy gravity.
A burden of fluttering wings
pinned into stillness.

Pinch the thorax
long chambered hearts
run the length of this body.
Inside forgiveness has grown tall.

Place it in a box
close the lid, walk away.
Sense a shadow that stills
half a moment after you stop.

A brief radiance kicks against the darkness

We are thick as thieves,
lifting pocket-watch moments
from the waistcoat of time.

These hours that belong to others
who wait impatiently for our will
to bend forming rigid shapes.

Lingering long in the heat
seeping from unlocked doors
until we feel the need of each other.

The crosshairs of our senses twitch,
we are hares nibbling on sun-
downing air carrying news of foxes.

Silhouettes sprint to the water's edge
setting sail on relentless cresting waves
knowing others will come aboard,
to cast shadows on an ocean we set alight.

Scenes from Summer

On the beach alone
rapt in our own voices
easing back and forth
across sand between us.
The sun basks in me,
draws me close to you.

The summer's plot
is ours to tend or untie.
Stirred by the shiver
of an early sunset
we drive to a village
seeking food and light.

We cajole a barman
into making us coffee.
In return we share
the warmth we own
waiting for clams
to ease open in the kitchen.

etna

offends the blue canopy
her rupture unresolving,
obscurer of man's ascent
hidden
by light-leeching plumage
the dull shade of a badly
laundered communion dress.

amid the uniformed purity
of a child's processional,
girls step in line
behind
their fathers and uncles.
above veiled children
men hoist a marble virgin.

stumbling as her bulk
breaks their sure stride,
broad backs perspiring
from lack of practice.
secrets
whispered by daughters
inside soft steepled hands.

Travelling Light

Everywhere I look there is the chance of new adventure
I hear your delight as darting sprats whisper on my skin
yet you are missing from this page of the photo album.

Ever the vigilant mother I watch as someone else's child
veers far too close to the main street. I am ready to react
love and exhaustion bind me into the spine of this story.

I fidget and fail to settle, shaking sand and restlessness
out from my towel, arms outstretched I am the colossal
Redeemer who stands high atop Mount Corcovado.

I watch another wrap her child in cotton softened by the sun
until the slippery four-limbed fish escapes into my heart
swollen and misshapen, pushing hard against my frame.

Field Dressing

I am meat
Not dry, hung, raw

I am the instant
beast's name becomes noun

muscle, fat and bone
unfasten from my skin.

The Macellaio tilts
a knife in his palm
rocking the blade's belly

tip right then left
ticking a counter movement
he advances across my surface.

Flare

Bile splashes into the bathtub,
he finally accepts this as proof

The Black kite drifts eternally
buoyed by Koan thermals.

that you are staying put today,
spoiling the jeep safari.

His span as wide as you are tall
wings not black but auburn alula.

Your body unmasks a flaw
that flexes the fist holding you.

The Black kite chases bonfire smoke
gathering up the smouldering twigs.

Celebrate the drumming
rebellion in your heart,

The Black kite flushes out his prey
drops embers on his target's home.

shower, dress, pack,
throw the keys under a clay pot.

The Black kite sets crops ablaze,
scorches the earth, burns bridges.

Feel your shape become solid
fired in the kiln of Aegean sun.

Boarding the SS Cameronia from Derry to New York (1912)

Pa pushes a punt into my hand
dry coarseness of his skin
stutters across my palm,
he feels like morning chores.
Around a prosperity of paper
Pa presses my hands together

he is closing his prayer book.
I feel the stain of a watermark
scarce, solemnity of a promise
protruding from my fingers.
Pa leans forward to kiss me
my shoulders stiffen in surprise

folding his razor cut lips inward
he withdraws, his neck flushing.
Notes stir in my open hand
I unfurl in the dockside wind.
I fear I will only see him again
in the solitude of his penmanship.

The Widow

Bridget's blouse buttons to her chin
the skin above her full, high breasts
will never freckle in the sun again.
Birthed five babies
nursed just three.
Over the eternal beds of two,
she prayed with new agnostic anger,
her white-knuckled fist refused
to scatter earth over her fruit.

Now here, dressed in black again,
her sister packs away a best dress.
Its burst of bright blue
is a Kingfisher's mantle
kindling her hair to a brash, bright red.
Sister reaches for her wedding gown
Bridget moves quickly across the room,
a lone rook on a chess board
undoing her sister's endgame with a look.

Sister fills her mouth with metal grips,
takes possession of Bridget's hair
gives her one last push into the shadows.
She binds it too tightly,
an angry rider fitting a horse's bridle.
Bridget's curls fight against the pull
skin taut at her temples.
She raises her head up towards the pain
thinking of him, tilting her chin to his lips.

Eisenhower's Secret Visit (May 1944)

The Fermanagh country road stirs and wakes
to the rumble of jeeps and the beat of boots.
Sat on a gate holding tight to the timber
waiting in thrall for the advent of the new.

Powerful arms swing past my smiling eyes
chevrons crumpling softly on khaki cloth.
Stiff and regimented, three hundred clock pendula
regulate a new and better time with their arrival.

I shine a fulsome beam as they rouse the rain
a downpour of silver strikes the floor.
Sweet blue and pink drops fall into my lap
bringing enchantment to my worn-out world.

I grab the candy cloudburst stuffing my pinafore pockets
laughing and cheering the soldiers greet me like a queen
I wave to my knights, here to hurl snakes back into the sea.

A Son (1978)

Watching a man raise his ▮▮ towards
the head of a young lad
crouching, covering his ▮▮
stills the rebel song inside me.

A second man points the double-barrel
shape of his power towards my ▮▮.
▮▮▮▮ give him licence to play sport
whilst the real threat to his life waits.

Cries of '▮▮' are strangled by the threat
of hands on a newly ripe Adam's Apple.
Tongues swollen fat with unsaid vitriol
push against our ▮▮ we cannot breathe.

▮▮▮▮ burns, marks adolescent bodies.
Leaves ▮▮ wounded
Leaves me ▮▮▮
▮▮▮ me no choices.

From nowhere the Sergeant's voice
strikes a final bell inside the hollow cup
bringing his officers to attention.
Ending their ▮▮.

A Father (1978)

A good father waits up by a low fire
tended by a working man
ready for his bed three hours since,

(...where the royal drums did beat)

His front bay window opens onto
the most beautiful, brutal view.
The liquid line of the Lough
shivers under the confrontational
shadow of the Queen's barracks.

(...and each and every night)

A father has a right to pace the floor,
a boy is still your boy
until he leaves his childhood home.

(Come out ye! black and tans!)

He has no whiskey in the house
a bare wooden chair steadies him.
Listening for a key hitting the lock,
metal clashing metal.

(...come out and fight me like a man,)

Silence, ungodly silence.

God in heaven let no uniform
knock at my door this night.

Silence (circa 1979)

My mother found silence oppressive. Her voice was strong,
commanding an army of acolytes.
It was distinct - so friends told me.
They said her language was different to my father's.
Her intonation rose above our flat Northern vowels,
soft hillocks cresting, falling through the terrain of her emotions

        when grenades of secrets were passed around
        her sound dipped low as a turf trench –
        pulling the pin before shock slackened mouths.

She was born by clear streams that gift her land an ever
dew grass, escaping or perhaps
rushing towards abundant isles.
Today her voice is stilled. The unspoken brings
expansion to a silence that I, as a child, could fill
with new sounds. Inside my ears I hear a torrent. I do not know

        this is the sound of a brook dammed with batons,
        rifles and bomb debris washed up from Home –
        breaching towards my mother.

To a River Spirit

I wobble a little in my stocking-feet
with each stroke of her perfumed wrist
my mother pulls stray strands tight
gathering up towards my first crown.

My father peeks around the door
to admire his woven child gift-
wrapped in red and golden silk
across the equator of his world.

Reaching down to correct my posture
his smile is the curve of my spine.

Wriggling free from inspection
I race him to the kitchen
rolling my stubby shoulders
I am the river spirit navigating

gateaux la cire onward to the feast.
We taste the honey on our hands

shiny, wax packages illuminating
the child that was my father,
still holding inside the echo
of a distant drum crescendo.

Waiting up for my Daughter

(After Caroline Bird)

I have her eyes. I hold them in my gaping mouth.
Feeling too high on his neck for a pulse, his bristles
cast a four o'clock shadow that scratch at her distress.
Too much pressure and panic fingerprint his throat.
The shirt on his back soaks in the concrete, asphalt,
flagstones, cobblestones and stains of Peterloo. She
kneels beside him. My tights ladder an hour away.
I swear an oath under my breath. Doormen hurl
a hardness of hailstones icing the scene, snow
drifting the truth into a picaresque adventure.
His brain, a wet cable, sparks before finally
disassociating from the mains. Doormen reach
into their tobacco pouches, fat fingers and thumbs
daintily pick out fragments binding the render
that walls in their apathy. Everyone is fighting
the urge to flee from the spiked kids that litter
at their feet. Blithe passers-by ignore the depetaling
of pale roses. Rotten marrow men swollen by untaxed
muscle and inertia spit out the hope of an easy night.
Another bell clangs against their temple. They lower
the velvet rope to let the sirens inside. Slipping
the night's purse into their pocket. Bleeding for no one.

The Principle of Succession

She says she is not my rock
and this is as it should be.
I, a craftsman
her lapidary
pick my tools blindly.

She has grown faceted,
dull, heavy, gritstone hewn.
Fear that belongs to others
strikes flint against flint

why did she not make fire?

She is the founding stone
long laid down.
Nothing has the force
to push her into a new form.

The hand glass of the sun
shifts darkness on her sundial.
Hold her long in your palm

she will mimic your warmth.

The Vote

(After Louis MacNeice)

Lady Justice falters, the end of a long week balancing the scales,
Judges' wigs hide halos, robes skim snaking silhouettes of tails,
I ponder the same old points of law as my key provokes the car
I haggle over morality like a tourist at a hellish bazaar;
I have a duty and a mortgage so my soul succumbs easily now,
how can I alone disassemble hate's apparatus anyhow.
I rev again impatiently flooding gas, cranking too fast
This is not the dream I conjured in low-lit libraries of my past,
I am unsuited to betraying good souls that fail to heal with time
and drive to sweet Gethsemane to deliver words of broken rhyme.
The blindfold slips to cover her mouth, the Lady can no longer respire
she died in spirit centuries ago, did you think she would never tire,
through every extortion, acquittal and release the wily advocate secures
Mercy dissolves like Lot's wife; just the grimace of her mouth endures.

Of Negligence

Dad draws breath reserving his lungs
to take a last plunge.

The doctor's gaze is steady,
a middle-class man looking

at a not middle-class man
who will not like his answer.

Still, he allows the man
to ask his hopeful question.

He could have been a medic, left school at fourteen. Takes more than one man's
wage to keep two houses, two maiden aunts; left on the shelf lost beneath the
obligations of others. He finds later in life his hands can heal,

draw pain away. Here he is, a poultice warming hard rolling pin shins stretched
on some invisible rack. Spasms blading through his five year old. He waits out
the hours listening to unsteady sobs, the gritting of milk teeth.

The doctor shifts behind his desk
reaching out his hand to signal
he is uncomfortable with the direction

of the conversation they did not have.

Meeting Bartholdi's Secret Muse

The corporal spoke with such patriotism that I recall him not in his uniform but draped in Lone Star red, white and blue silk sliding across his newly shaven cheek like a secret unravelling too quickly. The buttress of his cheekbones fluting upwards directing me to the seventeen sapphires of his eyes. A true Southern gent, he left as his Captain approached to walk me home through a deserted Paduan square. Seventy-eight fearsome statues, all patrician men floodlit into a forever daylight and one empty plinth. *He is impatient to unveil his muse, to conquer America.* In the dark I dream of the Captain dressing his handsome corporal, arranging his regal robes, guiding him like a father to stand still, to reach ever skyward with his burning torch. A sculptor approaches the scene, he kneels to place broken chains at the feet of the corporal rising to instruct his muse to bow in one final moment of humility to receive the radiant crown. Plaster white hands graze along fine bones that almost breach the skin, the sculptor lingers, tucking in imaginary loose locks.

Caught in Traffic

Light bleeds onto us from a Basilica
a consequence of women's inequality
we cross an intersection to the new town.
there is no way to make it safe.

Girls beached on traffic islands,
The abolitionist position favoured by feminists
step aside as we disembark from the road.

Titian carelessly abandoned sacred and profane
love at a dual carriageway on the Veneto
rejects the sanitising description "sex worker."

Something clutches at my womb
a form of violence in a neoliberal world
forcing a benign smile to Twin Venuses.

Looking directly at her breach's decorum
viewed as a commodity, like a burger.
a solecism, Nabokov would later explain.

The Untaken Photograph

Gianna yells across the black field, I can barely see her.
Red glowing paper singes my fingers, I swear softly.
She rolls tobacco like she makes cannoli,
too loosely folded with an overgenerous filling.
Gianna reports that the amp has died, she holds it aloft,
the moon reflects water dripping from the cable
crackling ominously,
it is the silence before a wartime radio broadcast.
We all yell back, *"drop the amp!"*
Gianna agrees, still gripping the handle
tensely telling us how her brother is going to kill her,
how he will enjoy doing it.

Around her the air alights.

I remember what we have been smoking and so hesitate
before I point to the air and ask, '...*what is this?*'
Lucciole! her eyes widen with delight, *Lucciole!*
I look at her blankly.
Gianna yells, "*Come si dice Lucciole in inglese?*"
"*Firefly!*" Max returns, emphatically flicking his teeth lisping on his lips.

We hold the moment, our hands in each other's watching the lucent pageant
as beetle beacons invite a mate to join them in the spotlight.
Clinging to each other, we are Arthur Conan Doyle, young Frances and Elsie
carrying their Midg camera down Cottingley Beck to 'tice the dancing Fairies.

Odium

Scraping mud onto a welcome mat
locals convulse behind white voile
at the sight of a biracial couple.
We double-lock the door
hear a gurgling beyond the walls,
a death rattle weakly respiring
into the first day of a new century.
Elders rush to hook two-pin plugs
up to the old machinery of hate.
A dusty Il Duce broods approval
amongst the family portraits.

The language barrier gifts a blissful
ignorance as jingoistic notes crawl
under our door into hands of friends.
Voltaire detains this lexis inside
his silken banyan pocket,
politely declining to translate.
Bertrand skilfully diverts us
with pacifism and dry pastries.

Rylands

*Cuneiform is one of the oldest forms of writing distinguished
by wedge shaped marks on clay tablets using a reed stylus.*

I lay out relics as if upon an altar, box after box,
corners smoothed with age, all a neat fit
for callous-free palms tasked with bringing
light into the dark mines of our ancient past.

The researcher steeples his hands and greets
his artefacts with the humility of an apostle.
He carefully prises the lid from one sand coloured box
the vacuum of time unseals with an unfamiliar whisper.

We withdraw our breath in wonder as Sumerian sands
exhale their enigmas into the climate-controlled room.
For a moment, this privilege suspends between us
like the updraft of a warm breeze on a falling feather.

He passes me a Cuneiform, I softly 'coo' like a bird,
building meaning with 'knee' and 'form.'
My cheeks flush at my own ignorance
as he responds with a 'Q,' a 'nuh' and a 'fawm.'

A dense weight of words imprint ciphers onto my hand.
I imagine fresh clay stockpiling speech from a reed's tip
to form imprints shaped like a tight-lipped mouth
or the narrowing eyes of a wily bondsman.

He thanks me for excavating treasure from the stacks
where oxygen starved rooms prolong these lives of clay.
He solemnly narrates to me the story of a mother
her soul sickened as she barters with a slave master

buying her two sons for twenty shekels of silver,
two lives freed four thousand years ago.
I nod at his translation as if I too can narrate
stories from these puzzling, naïve indents

I slip the clay back into his cradling hands,
he is lost in appraisal of early literate history.
Lives lived in Umma, her ancient civilisation
travelling alongside him, entrusting her truth.

NOTES & ACKNOWLEDGEMENTS

'St Francis' satyr' Published in *Consilience Journal*. Issue 10. 2022.
'A Son (1978)' For Sean.
'A Father (1978)' In memory of Uncle Johnny.
Lyrics in italics from 'Come out, Ye Black and Tans' by Dominic Behan.
'Silence (circa 1979)'. From *A Collection of Poems by Will Harris and Friends*.
'To a River Spirit' Dedicated to Melanie.
'Waiting up for my Daughter' After the Caroline Bird poem, 'Sanity'.
2020.
'The Principle of Succession' Published in *aAh! Magazine*. December
2020.
'The Vote' Published as 'The Senate Vote to Impeach', in *aAh! Magazine*.
March 2021. After the Louis MacNeice poem 'Sunday Morning' (1935).
'Meeting Bartholdi's Secret Muse' The sculptor and painter Frédéric
Auguste Bartholdi (1834-1904) designed The Statue of Liberty.
'Caught in Traffic' Words in italics from: *Decriminalisation of the sex trade
benefits pimps and brothel-owners, not women*. Julie Bindel. October 2017. *The
Guardian Online*.
'The Untaken Photograph.' For Lucio.
'Odium.' For Savio.

Huge thanks to MMU writers, Jane, Elspeth, Peter, Gayathri, Darcy, Susie,
Favour, Grae, Lauren, Sally, Julie and Josephine. To James, Helen, Adam,
Jean, Michael and Carol Ann at The Manchester Writing School, for
teaching me. To Sean Henderson, Chris Shum, Ivy Chow and Melanie
Lam for sharing stories. To the Henderson's and Karapalidis', especially
Jackie, Maria and Kay for keeping me connected to my heritage. To Lynn
and Catrina, Oksana and Selena for their positivity and encouragement.
To Eddie Thornton-Chan and Carolina Coppola for being the best part
of the NHS. To local poet, Paul R. and Marnie Devereux at Shorts Mag-
azine. Deepest gratitude to Jamie Hale, Peter Reynard, Romalyn Ante,
Ruth Harrison and Laura Kenwright at CRIPtic Arts and Spread the
Word. To Stuart Bartholemew at Verve Poetry Press for his patience and
kindness. To Mrs Mercer (nee Gaskill). To all the pupils and staff at my
School. To My Family.

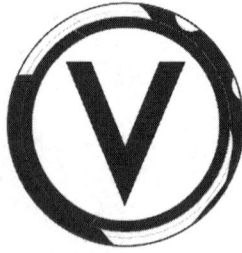

ABOUT VERVE POETRY PRESS

Verve Poetry Press is an award-winning press that focussed initially on meeting a local need in Birmingham - a need for the vibrant poetry scene here in Brum to find a way to present itself to the poetry world via publication. Co-founded by Stuart Bartholomew and Amerah Saleh, it now publishes poets from all corners of the UK and beyond - poets that speak to the city's varied and energetic qualities and will contribute to its many poetic stories.

Added to this is a colourful pamphlet series, many featuring poets who have performed at our sister festival - and a poetry show series which captures the magic of longer poetry performance pieces by festival alumni such as Polarbear, Matt Abbott and Imogen Stirling.

The press has been voted Most Innovative Publisher at the Saboteur Awards, and has won the Publisher's Award for Poetry Pamphlets at the Michael Marks Awards.

Like the festival, we strive to think about poetry in inclusive ways and embrace the multiplicity of approaches towards this glorious art.

https://vervepoetrypress.com
@VervePoetryPres
mail@vervepoetrypress.com